SOLAS

AMENDMENTS 2008 AND 2009

London, 2010

Published in 2010
by the INTERNATIONAL MARITIME ORGANIZATION
4 Albert Embankment, London SE1 7SR
www.imo.org

Printed in the United Kingdom by CPI Books Limited, Reading RG1 8EX

ISBN 978-92-801-1520-8

IMO PUBLICATION
Sales number: I175E

021019

Contents

[*] The amendments presented in this section were published in *SOLAS: 2006 Amendments*. The amendments are not included in *SOLAS, Consolidated edition 2009*, which incorporates amendments in effect as from 1 July 2009.

Page

Foreword

This publication contains the amendments to the International Convention for the Safety of Life at Sea (SOLAS) 1974 and to its 1988 Protocol that were adopted by the Maritime Safety Committee (MSC) in 2008 and 2009.

Resolution MSC.256(84) was adopted in May 2008 by the MSC at its eighty-fourth session and contains amendments to SOLAS chapters II-1, II-2, III, IV and the appendix including, in particular, new mandatory requirements for emergency towing on tankers and protection of vehicle, special category and ro–ro spaces.

Resolution MSC.257(84) was also adopted by the MSC at its eighty-fourth session in May 2008 and amends SOLAS chapter XI-1 to expand on SOLAS regulation I/21 and make parts I and II of the Code of International Standards and Recommended Practices for a Safety Investigation into a Marine Casualty or Marine Incident (Casualty Investigation Code) mandatory.

Resolution MSC.258(84), also adopted by the MSC at its eighty-fourth session in May 2008, amends the 1988 SOLAS Protocol, in particular modifying the records of equipment that are associated with several certificates.

Resolution MSC.269(85), which was adopted in December 2008 by the MSC at its eighty-fifth session, has two annexes. Annex 1 amends SOLAS chapters II-1 and II-2, taking into account the new mandatory and recommendatory stability requirements of the International Code on Intact Stability, 2008 (2008 IS Code). Annex 2 amends SOLAS chapters II-2, VI and VII, in matters pertaining to solid bulk cargoes, and, in particular, the International Maritime Solid Bulk Cargoes (IMSBC) Code adopted by the MSC by resolution MSC.268(85), and contains provisions on matters pertaining to the transport of dangerous goods.

Resolution MSC.282(86) was adopted in June 2009 by the MSC at its eighty-sixth session and contains amendments to SOLAS chapters II-1, V, VI and the appendix certificates. These amendments concern, in part, such navigation systems as the bridge navigational watch alarm system (BNWAS) and electronic chart display and information system (ECDIS).

Also adopted by the MSC at its eighty-sixth session in June 2009 was **resolution MSC.283(86)**, which amends the 1988 Protocol, modifying records of equipment associated with appendix certificates to account for the BNWAS.

Subject to the "tacit acceptance" procedure, these amendments entered into force, or are expected to enter into force, on:

.1 1 January 2010, for the amendments to the SOLAS 1974 Convention in resolution MSC.256(84) and resolution MSC.257(84) and for the amendments to the appendix to the 1988 SOLAS Protocol in resolution MSC.258(84);

.2 1 July 2010, for the amendments to the SOLAS 1974 Convention set out in annex 1 to resolution MSC.269(85); and

.3 1 January 2011, for the amendments to the SOLAS 1974 Convention set out in annex 2 to resolution MSC.269(85) and in resolution MSC.282(86) and for the amendments to the appendix to the 1988 SOLAS Protocol in resolution MSC.283(86).

Also presented are amendments comprising the annexes to resolutions MSC.201(81) and MSC.204(81), adopted in May 2006, and annex 3 to MSC.216(82), adopted in December 2006. These amendments were published in *SOLAS: 2006 Amendments* and are not included in *SOLAS, Consolidated edition 2009*, which incorporates amendments in effect as from 1 July 2009. The amendments in annex 3 concern, in part, new provisions related to passenger ship safety, including the new mandatory requirements related to the safe return to port concept, requirements for approving alternative designs and arrangements and safety centres, which will enter into force on 1 July 2010.

Footnotes in this publication have been added for ease of reference and do not form part of the SOLAS 1974 Convention or of its 1988 Protocol.

Amendments, by SOLAS chapter

Chapter	Resolution	Page in publication
I General provisions	MSC.204(81)	11
II-1 Construction – Structure, subdivision and stability, machinery and electrical installations	MSC.216(82) (annex 3) MSC.256(84) MSC.269(85) (annex 1) MSC.282(86)	15–17 33–35 53–54 69
II-2 Construction – Fire protection, fire detection and fire extinction	MSC.201(81) MSC.216(82) (annex 3) MSC.256(84) MSC.269(85) (annexes 1 and 2)	5 17–25 35–37 54–61
III Life-saving appliances and arrangements	MSC.201(81) MSC.216(82) (annex 3) MSC.256(84)	6 26–28 38–39
IV Radiocommunications	MSC.201(81) MSC.256(84)	6–7 39
V Safety of navigation	MSC.201(81) MSC.282(86)	7–8 70–72, 74
VI Carriage of cargoes	MSC.269(85) (annex 2) MSC.282(86)	61–63 72
VII Carriage of dangerous goods	MSC.269(85) (annex 2)	64
XI-1 Special measures to enhance maritime safety	MSC.257(84)	45

(continued)

Amendments, by SOLAS chapter *(concluded)*

Chapter	Resolution	Page in publication
Appendix Certificates	MSC.256(84)	39–41
	MSC.258(84)	49–50
	MSC.282(86)	73
	MSC.283(86)	77–78

2006 amendments

The amendments presented in this section comprise the annexes to resolutions MSC.201(81) and MSC.204(81), adopted in May 2006, and annex 3 to MSC.216(82), adopted in December 2006, and were published in *SOLAS: 2006 Amendments*. The amendments are not included in *SOLAS, Consolidated edition 2009*, which incorporates amendments in effect as from 1 July 2009. See the individual resolutions for information on the respective amendments' acceptance and entry into force.

Resolution MSC.201(81)

(adopted on 18 May 2006)

Adoption of amendments to the International Convention for the Safety of Life at Sea, 1974, as amended

THE MARITIME SAFETY COMMITTEE,

RECALLING Article 28(b) of the Convention on the International Maritime Organization concerning the functions of the Committee,

RECALLING FURTHER article VIII(b) of the International Convention for the Safety of Life at Sea (SOLAS), 1974 (hereinafter referred to as "the Convention"), concerning the amendment procedure applicable to the Annex to the Convention, other than the provisions of chapter I thereof,

HAVING CONSIDERED, at its eighty-first session, amendments to the Convention, proposed and circulated in accordance with article VIII(b)(i) thereof,

1. ADOPTS, in accordance with article VIII(b)(iv) of the Convention, amendments to the Convention, the text of which is set out in the annex to the present resolution;

2. DETERMINES, in accordance with article VIII(b)(vi)(2)(bb) of the Convention, that the said amendments shall be deemed to have been accepted on 1 January 2010, unless, prior to that date, more than one third of the Contracting Governments to the Convention or Contracting Governments the combined merchant fleets of which constitute not less than 50% of the gross tonnage of the world's merchant fleet, have notified their objections to the amendments;

3. INVITES SOLAS Contracting Governments to note that, in accordance with article VIII(b)(vii)(2) of the Convention, the amendments shall enter into force on 1 July 2010 upon their acceptance in accordance with paragraph 2 above;

4. REQUESTS the Secretary-General, in conformity with article VIII(b)(v) of the Convention, to transmit certified copies of the present resolution and the text of the amendments contained in the annex to all Contracting Governments to the Convention;

5. FURTHER REQUESTS the Secretary-General to transmit copies of this resolution and its annex to Members of the Organization which are not Contracting Governments to the Convention.

Annex

Amendments to the International Convention for the Safety of Life at Sea, 1974, as amended

Chapter II-2
Construction – Fire protection, fire detection and fire extinction

Regulation 9
Containment of fire

1 *In subparagraph .2 of paragraph 4.1.3.3, "." is replaced by* "; or".

2 *In paragraph 4.1.3.3, the following new subparagraph .3 is added after the existing subparagraph .2:*

> "**.3** water-mist nozzles that have been tested and approved in accordance with the guidelines approved by the Organization.*

* Refer to the Revised Guidelines for approval of sprinkler systems equivalent to that referred to in SOLAS regulation II-2/12 (resolution A.800(19))."

Regulation 15
*Arrangements for oil fuel, lubricating oil and other flammable oils**

3 *In regulation II-2/15, as amended by resolution MSC.31(63), the text after the title is replaced by the following:*

"(Paragraphs 2.9 to 2.12 of this regulation apply to ships constructed on or after 1 February 1992, except that the references to paragraphs 2.10 and 2.11 in paragraphs 3 and 4 apply to ships constructed on or after 1 July 1998)".

* Refer to *SOLAS, Consolidated Edition 2001,* ISBN 92-801-5100-2, IMO sales number IC110E.

Chapter III
Life-saving appliances and arrangements

Regulation 7
Personal life-saving appliances

4 *In paragraph 2.1, the following new subparagraphs .1 and .2 are inserted:*

"**.1** for passenger ships on voyages of less than 24 hours, a number of infant lifejackets equal to at least 2.5% of the number of passengers on board shall be provided;

.2 for passenger ships on voyages of 24 hours or greater, infant lifejackets shall be provided for each infant on board;",

and the existing subparagraphs .1 and .2 are renumbered as subparagraphs .3 and .4. The word "and" *is moved from the end of renumbered subparagraph .3 to the end of renumbered subparagraph .4.*

5 *The following new subparagraph .5 is inserted after the renumbered subparagraph .4 of paragraph 2.1:*

"**.5** if the adult lifejackets provided are not designed to fit persons weighing up to 140 kg and with a chest girth of up to 1,750 mm, a sufficient number of suitable accessories shall be available on board to allow them to be secured to such persons."

Chapter IV
Radiocommunications

Regulation 7
Radio equipment: General

6 *The existing text of subparagraph .6.1 of paragraph 1 is replaced by the following:*

"**.6.1** capable of transmitting a distress alert through the polar orbiting satellite service operating in the 406 MHz band;"

Regulation 9
Radio equipment: Sea areas A1 and A2

7 *The existing text of subparagraph .3.3 of paragraph 1 is replaced by the following:*

> ".**3.3** through the Inmarsat geostationary satellite service by a ship earth station."

Regulation 10
Radio equipment: Sea areas A1, A2 and A3

8 *The existing text of subparagraph .4.3 of paragraph 1 is replaced by the following:*

> ".**4.3** through the Inmarsat geostationary satellite service by an additional ship earth station."

9 *The existing text of subparagraph .3.2 of paragraph 2 is replaced by the following:*

> ".**3.2** through the Inmarsat geostationary satellite service by a ship earth station; and"

Chapter V
Safety of navigation

Regulation 22
Navigation bridge visibility

10 *The following new paragraph 4 is added after the existing paragraph 3:*

"**4** Notwithstanding the requirements of paragraphs 1.1, 1.3, 1.4 and 1.5, ballast water exchange may be undertaken provided that:

.1 the master has determined that it is safe to do so and takes into consideration any increased blind sectors or reduced horizontal fields of vision resulting from the operation to ensure that a proper lookout is maintained at all times;

.2 the operation is conducted in accordance with the ship's ballast water management plan, taking into account the recommendations on ballast water exchange adopted by the Organization; and

.3 the commencement and termination of the operation are recorded in the ship's record of navigational activities pursuant to regulation 28."

Resolution MSC.204(81)
(adopted on 18 May 2006)

Adoption of amendments to the Protocol of 1988 relating to the International Convention for the Safety of Life at Sea, 1974

THE MARITIME SAFETY COMMITTEE,

RECALLING Article 28(b) of the Convention on the International Maritime Organization concerning the functions of the Committee,

RECALLING ALSO article VIII(b) of the International Convention for the Safety of Life at Sea, 1974 (hereinafter referred to as "the Convention") and article VI of the Protocol of 1988 relating to the Convention (hereinafter referred to as "the 1988 SOLAS Protocol") concerning the procedure for amending the Convention and the 1988 SOLAS Protocol,

RECALLING FURTHER article VI(b) of the 1988 SOLAS Protocol which stipulates, *inter alia,* that amendments to the Annex to the Protocol shall be adopted and brought into force in accordance with the procedure applicable to the adoption and entry into force of amendments to chapter I of the Annex to the Convention, as specified in subparagraphs (iv), (vi)(1) and (vii)(1) of paragraph (b) of article VIII of the Convention,

NOTING that, in accordance with article VIII(b)(vi)(1) of the Convention, an amendment to the Annex to the 1988 SOLAS Protocol shall be deemed to have been accepted on the date on which it is accepted by two thirds of the Parties to the Protocol,

HAVING CONSIDERED, at its eighty-first session, amendments to the 1988 SOLAS Protocol proposed and circulated in accordance with article VIII(b)(i) of the Convention and article VI(b) of the 1988 SOLAS Protocol,

1. ADOPTS, in accordance with article VIII(b)(iv) of the Convention and article VI(b) of the 1988 SOLAS Protocol, amendments to the Annex to the 1988 SOLAS Protocol, the text of which is set out in the annex to the present resolution;

2. REQUESTS the Secretary-General, in accordance with article VIII(b)(v) of the Convention and article VI(b) of the 1988 SOLAS Protocol, to transmit certified copies of the present resolution and its annex to all Parties to the 1988 SOLAS Protocol, for consideration and acceptance, and also to transmit copies to all Members of the Organization;

3. URGES all Parties to the 1988 SOLAS Protocol to accept the amendments at the earliest possible date.

Annex

Amendments to the Protocol of 1988 relating to the International Convention for the Safety of Life at Sea, 1974

Annex

Modifications and additions to the Annex to the International Convention for the Safety of Life at Sea, 1974

Chapter I *General provisions*

Part B
Surveys and certificates

Regulation 10
Surveys of structure, machinery and equipment of cargo ships

The existing text of subparagraph (v) of paragraph (a) of the regulation is replaced by the following:

"**(v)** a minimum of two inspections of the outside of the ship's bottom during the five-year period of validity of the Cargo Ship Safety Construction Certificate or the Cargo Ship Safety Certificate, except where regulation 14(e) or 14(f) is applicable. Where regulation 14(e) or 14(f) is applicable, this five-year period may be extended to coincide with the extended period of validity of the certificate. In all cases the interval between any two such inspections shall not exceed 36 months;".

Resolution MSC.216(82)

(adopted on 8 December 2006)

Amendments to the International Convention for the Safety of Life at Sea, 1974, as amended

THE MARITIME SAFETY COMMITTEE,

RECALLING Article 28(b) of the Convention on the International Maritime Organization concerning the functions of the Committee,

RECALLING FURTHER article VIII(b) of the International Convention for the Safety of Life at Sea (SOLAS), 1974 (hereinafter referred to as "the Convention"), concerning the amendment procedure applicable to the Annex to the Convention, other than to the provisions of chapter I thereof,

HAVING CONSIDERED, at its eighty-second session, amendments to the Convention, proposed and circulated in accordance with article VIII(b)(i) thereof,

1. ADOPTS, in accordance with article VIII(b)(iv) of the Convention, amendments to the Convention, the text of which is set out in annexes 1, 2 and 3 to the present resolution;

2. DETERMINES, in accordance with article VIII(b)(vi)(2)(bb) of the Convention, that:

(a) the said amendments, set out in annex 1, shall be deemed to have been accepted on 1 January 2008;*

(b) the said amendments, set out in annex 2, shall be deemed to have been accepted on 1 July 2008;* and

(c) the said amendments, set out in annex 3, shall be deemed to have been accepted on 1 January 2010,

unless, prior to those dates, more than one third of the Contracting Governments to the Convention or Contracting Governments the

* The amendments in this annex have been incorporated in *SOLAS, Consolidated edition 2009*, and are not presented in this publication.

combined merchant fleets of which constitute not less than 50% of the gross tonnage of the world's merchant fleet, have notified their objections to the amendments;

3. INVITES SOLAS Contracting Governments to note that, in accordance with article VIII(b)(vii)(2) of the Convention:

(a) the amendments, set out in annex 1, shall enter into force on 1 July 2008;

(b) the amendments, set out in annex 2, shall enter into force on 1 January 2009; and

(c) the amendments, set out in annex 3, shall enter into force on 1 July 2010,

upon their acceptance in accordance with paragraph 2 above;

4. REQUESTS the Secretary-General, in conformity with article VIII(b)(v) of the Convention, to transmit certified copies of the present resolution and the text of the amendments contained in annexes 1, 2 and 3 to all Contracting Governments to the Convention;

5. FURTHER REQUESTS the Secretary-General to transmit copies of this resolution and its annexes 1, 2 and 3 to Members of the Organization which are not Contracting Governments to the Convention.

Annex 3

Amendments to the International Convention for the Safety of Life at Sea, 1974, as amended

Chapter II-1
Construction – Structure, subdivision and stability, machinery and electrical installations

Part D
Electrical installations

Regulation 41
Main source of electrical power and lighting systems

1 *The following new paragraph 6 is added after the existing paragraph 5:*

"**6** In passenger ships, supplementary lighting shall be provided in all cabins to clearly indicate the exit so that occupants will be able to find their way to the door. Such lighting, which may be connected to an emergency source of power or have a self-contained source of electrical power in each cabin, shall automatically illuminate when power to the normal cabin lighting is lost and remain on for a minimum of 30 minutes."

2 *The following new part F is added after the existing regulation 54:*

"Part F
Alternative design and arrangements

Regulation 55
Alternative design and arrangements

1 Purpose

The purpose of this regulation is to provide a methodology for alternative design and arrangements for machinery and electrical installations.

2 General

2.1 Machinery and electrical installation design and arrangements may deviate from the requirements set out in parts C, D and E, provided that the alternative design and arrangements meet the intent of the requirements concerned and provide an equivalent level of safety to this chapter.

2.2 When alternative design or arrangements deviate from the prescriptive requirements of parts C, D and E, an engineering analysis, evaluation and approval of the design and arrangements shall be carried out in accordance with this regulation.

3 Engineering analysis

The engineering analysis shall be prepared and submitted to the Administration, based on the guidelines developed by the Organization,* and shall include, as a minimum, the following elements:

.1 determination of the ship type, machinery, electrical installations and space(s) concerned;

.2 identification of the prescriptive requirement(s) with which the machinery and electrical installations will not comply;

.3 identification of the reason the proposed design will not meet the prescriptive requirements supported by compliance with other recognized engineering or industry standards;

.4 determination of the performance criteria for the ship, machinery, electrical installation or the space(s) concerned addressed by the relevant prescriptive requirement(s):

- **.4.1** performance criteria shall provide a level of safety not inferior to the relevant prescriptive requirements contained in parts C, D and E; and
- **.4.2** performance criteria shall be quantifiable and measurable;

.5 detailed description of the alternative design and arrangements, including a list of the assumptions used in the design and any proposed operational restrictions or conditions;

.6 technical justification demonstrating that the alternative design and arrangements meet the safety performance criteria; and

.7 risk assessment based on identification of the potential faults and hazards associated with the proposal.

* Refer to the Guidelines on alternative design and arrangements for SOLAS chapters II-1 and III (MSC.1/Circ.1212).

4 **Evaluation of the alternative design and arrangements**

4.1 The engineering analysis required in paragraph 3 shall be evaluated and approved by the Administration, taking into account the guidelines developed by the Organization.*

4.2 A copy of the documentation, as approved by the Administration, indicating that the alternative design and arrangements comply with this regulation shall be carried on board the ship.

5 **Exchange of information**

The Administration shall communicate to the Organization pertinent information concerning alternative design and arrangements approved by them for circulation to all Contracting Governments.

6 **Re-evaluation due to change of conditions**

If the assumptions and operational restrictions that were stipulated in the alternative design and arrangements are changed, the engineering analysis shall be carried out under the changed condition and shall be approved by the Administration.

* Refer to the Guidelines on alternative design and arrangements for SOLAS chapters II-1 and III (MSC.1/Circ.1212)."

Chapter II-2
Construction – Fire protection, fire detection and fire extinction

Regulation 3
Definitions

3 *The following new paragraphs 51 and 52 are added after the existing paragraph 50:*

"**51** *Safe area* in the context of a casualty is, from the perspective of habitability, any area(s) which is not flooded or which is outside the main vertical zone(s) in which a fire has occurred such that it can safely accommodate all persons on board to protect them from hazards to life or health and provide them with basic services.

52 *Safety centre* is a control station dedicated to the management of emergency situations. Safety systems' operation, control and/or monitoring are an integral part of the safety centre."

Regulation 7
Detection and alarm

4 *The following new paragraph 2.4 is added after the existing paragraph 2.3:*

"**2.4** A fixed fire detection and fire alarm system for passenger ships shall be capable of remotely and individually identifying each detector and manually operated call point."

5 *In paragraphs 5.2 and 5.3.1, the following new text is added at the end of the paragraphs:*

"Detectors fitted in cabins, when activated, shall also be capable of emitting, or cause to be emitted, an audible alarm within the space where they are located."

Regulation 8
Control of smoke spread

6 *In paragraph 2, the following new sentence is added at the end of the paragraph:*

"The ventilation system serving safety centres may be derived from the ventilation system serving the navigation bridge, unless located in an adjacent main vertical zone."

Regulation 9
Containment of fire

7 *In paragraph 2.2.3.2.2 (7), the words* "Sale shops" *are deleted.*

8 *In paragraph 2.2.3.2.2 (8), the words* "Sale shops" *are added.*

9 *In the notes for tables 9.3 and 9.4, the following sentence is added at the end of subscript "c":*

"No fire rating is required for those partitions separating the navigation bridge and the safety centre when the latter is within the navigation bridge."

10 *The following new paragraph 2.2.7 is added after paragraph 2.2.6:*

"**2.2.7** *Protection of atriums*

2.2.7.1 Atriums shall be within enclosures formed of "A" class divisions having a fire rating determined in accordance with tables 9.2 and 9.4, as applicable.

2.2.7.2 Decks separating spaces within atriums shall have a fire rating determined in accordance with tables 9.2 and 9.4, as applicable."

11 *The existing paragraph 7.5.1 is renumbered as paragraph 7.5.1.1 and the following new paragraph 7.5.1.2 is added thereafter:*

"**7.5.1.2** Exhaust ducts from ranges for cooking equipment installed on open decks shall conform to paragraph 7.5.1.1, as applicable, when passing through accommodation spaces or spaces containing combustible materials."

12 *The following new paragraph 7.6 is added after the existing paragraph 7.5.2.1:*

"**7.6** *Ventilation systems for main laundries in ships carrying more than 36 passengers*

Exhaust ducts from main laundries shall be fitted with:

.1 filters readily removable for cleaning purposes;

.2 a fire damper located in the lower end of the duct which is automatically and remotely operated;

.3 remote-control arrangements for shutting off the exhaust fans and supply fans from within the space and for operating the fire damper mentioned in paragraph 7.6.2; and

.4 suitably located hatches for inspection and cleaning."

Regulation 10
Fire fighting

13 *In the first sentence of paragraph 6.4, between the words* "equipment" *and* "shall", *the words* "installed in enclosed spaces or on open decks" *are added.*

Regulation 13
Means of escape

14 *In paragraph 3.2.3, the words* "public spaces" *in the third sentence are deleted and the following new sentence is added before the fourth sentence:*

"Public spaces may also have direct access to stairway enclosures except for the backstage of a theatre."

15 *The following new paragraph 3.2.5.3 is added after the existing paragraph 3.2.5.2:*

"**3.2.5.3** In lieu of the escape route lighting system required by paragraph 3.2.5.1, alternative evacuation guidance systems may be accepted if approved by the Administration based on the guidelines developed by the Organization.*

* Refer to the Functional requirements and performance standards for the assessment of evacuation guidance systems (MSC/Circ.1167) and the Interim guidelines for the testing, approval and maintenance of evacuation guidance systems used as an alternative to low-location lighting systems (MSC/Circ.1168)."

16 *The following new regulations 21, 22 and 23 are added after the existing regulation 20:*

"Regulation 21
Casualty threshold, safe return to port and safe areas

1 Application

Passenger ships constructed on or after 1 July 2010 having a length, as defined in regulation II-1/2.5, of 120 m or more or having three or more main vertical zones shall comply with the provisions of this regulation.

2 Purpose

The purpose of this regulation is to establish design criteria for a ship's safe return to port under its own propulsion after a casualty that does not exceed the casualty threshold stipulated in paragraph 3 and also provides functional requirements and performance standards for safe areas.

3 Casualty threshold

The casualty threshold, in the context of a fire, includes:

.1 loss of space of origin up to the nearest "A" class boundaries, which may be a part of the space of origin, if the space of origin is protected by a fixed fire-extinguishing system; or

.2 loss of the space of origin and adjacent spaces up to the nearest "A" class boundaries which are not part of the space of origin.

4 Safe return to port*

When fire damage does not exceed the casualty threshold indicated in paragraph 3, the ship shall be capable of returning to port while providing a safe area as defined in regulation 3.51. To be deemed capable of returning to port, the following systems shall remain operational in the remaining part of the ship not affected by fire:

.1 propulsion;

.2 steering systems and steering-control systems;

.3 navigational systems;

.4 systems for fill, transfer and service of fuel oil;

.5 internal communication between the bridge, engineering spaces, safety centre, fire-fighting and damage-control teams, and as required for passenger and crew notification and mustering;

.6 external communication;

.7 fire main system;

.8 fixed fire-extinguishing systems;

.9 fire and smoke detection system;

.10 bilge and ballast system;

.11 power-operated watertight and semi-watertight doors;

.12 systems intended to support "safe areas" as indicated in paragraph 5.1.2;

.13 flooding detection systems; and

---

* Refer to the Performance standards for the systems and services to remain operational on passenger ships for safe return to port and orderly evacuation and abandonment after a casualty (MSC.1/Circ.1214).

.14 other systems determined by the Administration to be vital to damage control efforts.

5 Safe area(s)

5.1 *Functional requirements:*

.1 the safe area(s) shall generally be an internal space(s); however, the use of an external space as a safe area may be allowed by the Administration taking into account any restriction due to the area of operation and relevant expected environmental conditions;

.2 the safe area(s) shall provide all occupants with the following basic services* to ensure that the health of passengers and crew is maintained:

.2.1 sanitation;

.2.2 water;

.2.3 food;

.2.4 alternate space for medical care;

.2.5 shelter from the weather;

.2.6 means of preventing heat stress and hypothermia;

.2.7 light; and

.2.8 ventilation;

.3 ventilation design shall reduce the risk of smoke and hot gases that could affect the use of the safe area(s); and

.4 means of access to life-saving appliances shall be provided from each area identified or used as a safe area, taking into account that a main vertical zone may not be available for internal transit.

5.2 *Alternate space for medical care*

Alternate space for medical care shall conform to a standard acceptable to the Administration.†

---

* Refer to the Performance standards for the systems and services to remain operational on passenger ships for safe return to port and orderly evacuation and abandonment after a casualty (MSC.1/Circ.1214).

† Refer to the Guidance on the establishment of medical and sanitation related programmes for passenger ships (MSC/Circ.1129).

Regulation 22
Design criteria for systems to remain operational after a fire casualty

1 Application

Passenger ships constructed on or after 1 July 2010 having a length, as defined in regulation II-1/2.5, of 120 m or more or having three or more main vertical zones shall comply with the provisions of this regulation.

2 Purpose

The purpose of this regulation is to provide design criteria for systems required to remain operational for supporting the orderly evacuation and abandonment of a ship, if the casualty threshold, as defined in regulation 21.3, is exceeded.

3 Systems*

3.1 In case any one main vertical zone is unserviceable due to fire, the following systems shall be so arranged and segregated as to remain operational:

.1 fire main;

.2 internal communications (in support of fire fighting as required for passenger and crew notification and evacuation);

.3 means of external communications;

.4 bilge systems for removal of fire-fighting water;

.5 lighting along escape routes, at assembly stations and at embarkation stations of life-saving appliances; and

.6 guidance systems for evacuation shall be available.

3.2 The above systems shall be capable of operation for at least 3 h based on the assumption of no damage outside the unserviceable main vertical zone. These systems are not required to remain operational within the unserviceable main vertical zones.

---

* Refer to the Performance standards for the systems and services to remain operational on passenger ships for safe return to port and orderly evacuation and abandonment after a casualty (MSC.1/Circ.1214).

3.3 Cabling and piping within a trunk constructed to an "A-60" standard shall be deemed to remain intact and serviceable while passing through the unserviceable main vertical zone for the purposes of paragraph 3.1. An equivalent degree of protection for cabling and piping may be approved by the Administration.

Regulation 23
Safety centre on passenger ships

1 Application

Passenger ships constructed on or after 1 July 2010 shall have on board a safety centre complying with the requirements of this regulation.

2 Purpose

The purpose of this regulation is to provide a space to assist with the management of emergency situations.

3 Location and arrangement

The safety centre shall either be a part of the navigation bridge or be located in a separate space adjacent, but having direct access, to the navigation bridge, so that the management of emergencies can be performed without distracting watch officers from their navigational duties.

4 Layout and ergonomic design

The layout and ergonomic design of the safety centre shall take into account the guidelines developed by the Organization,* as appropriate.

5 Communications

Means of communication between the safety centre, the central control station, the navigation bridge, the engine control room, the storage room(s) for fire-extinguishing system(s) and fire equipment lockers shall be provided.

* Refer to the guidelines to be developed by the Organization.

6 Control and monitoring of safety systems

Notwithstanding the requirements set out elsewhere in the Convention, the full functionality (operation, control, monitoring or any combination thereof, as required) of the safety systems listed below shall be available from the safety centre:

.1 all powered ventilation systems;

.2 fire doors;

.3 general emergency alarm system;

.4 public address system;

.5 electrically powered evacuation guidance systems;

.6 watertight and semi-watertight doors;

.7 indicators for shell doors, loading doors and other closing appliances;

.8 water leakage of inner/outer bow doors, stern doors and any other shell door;

.9 television surveillance system;

.10 fire detection and alarm system;

.11 fixed fire-fighting local application system(s);

.12 sprinkler and equivalent systems;

.13 water-based fire-extinguishing systems for machinery spaces;

.14 alarm to summon the crew;

.15 atrium smoke extraction system;

.16 flooding detection systems; and

.17 fire pumps and emergency fire pumps."

Chapter III
Life-saving appliances and arrangements

Regulation 4
Evaluation, testing and approval of life-saving appliances and arrangements

17 *Paragraph 3 is replaced by the following:*

"**3** Before giving approval to novel life-saving appliances or arrangements, the Administration shall ensure that such:

.1 appliances provide safety standards at least equivalent to the requirements of this chapter and the Code and have been evaluated and tested based on the guidelines developed by the Organization;* or

.2 arrangements have successfully undergone an engineering analysis, evaluation and approval in accordance with regulation 38.

* Refer to the guidelines to be developed by the Organization."

18 *The following new part C is added after the existing regulation 37:*

"Part C
Alternative design and arrangements

Regulation 38
Alternative design and arrangements

1 Purpose

The purpose of this regulation is to provide a methodology for alternative design and arrangements for life-saving appliances and arrangements.

2 General

2.1 Life-saving appliances and arrangements may deviate from the requirements set out in part B, provided that the alternative design and arrangements meet the intent of the requirements concerned and provide an equivalent level of safety to this chapter.

2.2 When alternative design or arrangements deviate from the prescriptive requirements of part B, an engineering analysis, evaluation and approval of the design and arrangements shall be carried out in accordance with this regulation.

3 Engineering analysis

The engineering analysis shall be prepared and submitted to the Administration, based on the guidelines developed by the Organization* and shall include, as a minimum, the following elements:

.1 determination of the ship type and the life-saving appliance and arrangements concerned;

.2 identification of the prescriptive requirement(s) with which the life-saving appliance and arrangements will not comply;

.3 identification of the reason the proposed design will not meet the prescriptive requirements supported by compliance with other recognized engineering or industry standards;

.4 determination of the performance criteria for the ship and the life-saving appliance and arrangements concerned addressed by the relevant prescriptive requirement(s):

  .4.1 performance criteria shall provide a level of safety not inferior to the relevant prescriptive requirements contained in part B; and

  .4.2 performance criteria shall be quantifiable and measurable;

.5 detailed description of the alternative design and arrangements, including a list of the assumptions used in the design and any proposed operational restrictions or conditions;

.6 technical justification demonstrating that the alternative design and arrangements meet the safety performance criteria; and

.7 risk assessment based on identification of the potential faults and hazards associated with the proposal.

---

* Refer to the Guidelines on alternative design and arrangements for SOLAS chapters II-1 and III (MSC.1/Circ.1212).

4 Evaluation of the alternative design and arrangements

4.1 The engineering analysis required in paragraph 3 shall be evaluated and approved by the Administration, taking into account the guidelines developed by the Organization.*

4.2 A copy of the documentation, as approved by the Administration, indicating that the alternative design and arrangements comply with this regulation, shall be carried on board the ship.

5 Exchange of information

The Administration shall communicate to the Organization pertinent information concerning alternative design and arrangements approved by them for circulation to all Contracting Governments.

6 Re-evaluation due to change of conditions

If the assumptions and operational restrictions that were stipulated in the alternative design and arrangements are changed, the engineering analysis shall be carried out under the changed condition and shall be approved by the Administration."

* Refer to the Guidelines on alternative design and arrangements for SOLAS chapters II-1 and III (MSC.1/Circ.1212).

2008 amendments

Resolution MSC.256(84)
(adopted on 16 May 2008)

Adoption of amendments to the International Convention for the Safety of Life at Sea, 1974, as amended

THE MARITIME SAFETY COMMITTEE,

RECALLING Article 28(b) of the Convention on the International Maritime Organization concerning the functions of the Committee,

RECALLING FURTHER article VIII(b) of the International Convention for the Safety of Life at Sea (SOLAS), 1974 (hereinafter referred to as "the Convention"), concerning the amendment procedure applicable to the Annex to the Convention, other than to the provisions of chapter I thereof,

HAVING CONSIDERED, at its eighty-fourth session, amendments to the Convention, proposed and circulated in accordance with article VIII(b)(i) thereof,

1. ADOPTS, in accordance with article VIII(b)(iv) of the Convention, amendments to the Convention, the text of which is set out in the annex to the present resolution;

2. DETERMINES, in accordance with article VIII(b)(vi)(2)(bb) of the Convention, that the said amendments shall be deemed to have been accepted on 1 July 2009, unless, prior to that date, more than one third of the Contracting Governments to the Convention or Contracting Governments the combined merchant fleets of which constitute not less than 50% of the gross tonnage of the world's merchant fleet, have notified their objections to the amendments;

3. INVITES SOLAS Contracting Governments to note that, in accordance with article VIII(b)(vii)(2) of the Convention, the amendments shall enter into force on 1 January 2010 upon their acceptance in accordance with paragraph 2 above;

4. RECOMMENDS the Contracting Governments concerned to issue certificates complying with the annexed amendments at the first renewal survey on or after 1 January 2010;

5. REQUESTS the Secretary-General, in conformity with article VIII(b)(v) of the Convention, to transmit certified copies of the present resolution and the text of the amendments contained in the annex to all Contracting Governments to the Convention;

6. FURTHER REQUESTS the Secretary-General to transmit copies of this resolution and its annex to Members of the Organization, which are not Contracting Governments to the Convention.

Annex

Amendments to the International Convention for the Safety of Life at Sea, 1974, as amended

Chapter II-1
Construction – Structure, subdivision and stability, machinery and electrical installations

Regulation 3-4
Emergency towing arrangements on tankers

1 *The existing regulation 3-4 is replaced by the following:*

"Regulation 3-4
Emergency towing arrangements and procedures

1 Emergency towing arrangements on tankers

1.1 Emergency towing arrangements shall be fitted at both ends on board every tanker of not less than 20,000 tonnes deadweight.

1.2 For tankers constructed on or after 1 July 2002:

.1 the arrangements shall, at all times, be capable of rapid deployment in the absence of main power on the ship to be towed and easy connection to the towing ship. At least one of the emergency towing arrangements shall be pre-rigged ready for rapid deployment; and

.2 emergency towing arrangements at both ends shall be of adequate strength taking into account the size and deadweight of the ship, and the expected forces during bad weather conditions. The design and construction and prototype testing of emergency towing arrangements shall be approved by the Administration, based on the guidelines developed by the Organization.*

* Refer to the Guidelines on emergency towing arrangements for tankers, adopted by the Maritime Safety Committee by resolution MSC.35(63), as amended.

1.3 For tankers constructed before 1 July 2002, the design and construction of emergency towing arrangements shall be approved by the Administration, based on the guidelines developed by the Organization.*

2 Emergency towing procedures on ships

2.1 This paragraph applies to:

.1 all passenger ships, not later than 1 January 2010;

.2 cargo ships constructed on or after 1 January 2010; and

.3 cargo ships constructed before 1 January 2010, not later than 1 January 2012.

2.2 Ships shall be provided with a ship-specific emergency towing procedure. Such a procedure shall be carried aboard the ship for use in emergency situations and shall be based on existing arrangements and equipment available on board the ship.

2.3 The procedure† shall include:

.1 drawings of fore and aft deck showing possible emergency towing arrangements;

.2 inventory of equipment on board that can be used for emergency towing;

.3 means and methods of communication; and

.4 sample procedures to facilitate the preparation for and conducting of emergency towing operations.

* Refer to the Guidelines on emergency towing arrangements for tankers, adopted by the Maritime Safety Committee by resolution MSC.35(63), as amended.

† Refer to the Guidelines for owners/operators on preparing emergency towing procedures (MSC.1/Circ.1255)."

2 *The following new regulation 3-9 is added after the existing regulation 3-8:*

"Regulation 3-9

Means of embarkation on and disembarkation from ships

1 Ships constructed on or after 1 January 2010 shall be provided with means of embarkation on and disembarkation from ships for use in port and in port-related operations, such as gangways and accommodation ladders, in accordance with paragraph 2, unless the Administration deems that compliance with a particular provision is unreasonable or impractical.*

2 The means of embarkation and disembarkation required in paragraph 1 shall be constructed and installed based on the guidelines developed by the Organization.†

3 For all ships the means of embarkation and disembarkation shall be inspected and maintained† in suitable condition for their intended purpose, taking into account any restrictions related to safe loading. All wires used to support the means of embarkation and disembarkation shall be maintained as specified in regulation III/20.4.

* Circumstances where compliance may be deemed unreasonable or impractical may include where the ship:

.1 has small freeboards and is provided with boarding ramps; or

.2 is engaged in voyages between designated ports where appropriate shore accommodation/embarkation ladders (platforms) are provided.

† Refer to the Guidelines for construction, installation, maintenance and inspection/survey of means of embarkation and disembarkation (MSC.1/Circ.1331)."

Chapter II-2
Construction – Fire protection, fire detection and fire extinction

Regulation 10
Fire fighting

3 *The following new paragraph 4.1.5 is added after the existing paragraph 4.1.4:*

"**4.1.5** By the first scheduled dry-docking after 1 January 2010, fixed carbon dioxide fire-extinguishing systems for the protection of machinery spaces and cargo pump-rooms on ships constructed before 1 July 2002 shall comply with the provisions of paragraph 2.2.2 of chapter 5 of the Fire Safety Systems Code."

Regulation 19
Carriage of dangerous goods

4 *In paragraph 4, the words* ", as defined in regulation VII/2," *are deleted.*

Regulation 20
Protection of vehicle, special category and ro–ro spaces

5 *The existing paragraph 6.1.4 is replaced by the following paragraph 6.1.4 and new paragraph 6.1.5 is added after paragraph 6.1.4 as follows:*

"**6.1.4** The requirement of this paragraph shall apply to ships constructed on or after 1 January 2010. Ships constructed on or after 1 July 2002 and before 1 January 2010 shall comply with the previously applicable requirements of paragraph 6.1.4, as amended by resolution MSC.99(73). When fixed pressure water-spraying systems are fitted, in view of the serious loss of stability which could arise due to large quantities of water accumulating on the deck or decks during the operation of the fixed pressure water-spraying system, the following arrangements shall be provided:

.1 in passenger ships:

.1.1 in the spaces above the bulkhead deck, scuppers shall be fitted so as to ensure that such water is rapidly discharged directly overboard, taking into account the guidelines developed by the Organization;*

.1.2.1 in ro–ro passenger ships, discharge valves for scuppers, fitted with positive means of closing operable from a position above the bulkhead deck in accordance with the requirements of the International Convention on Load Lines in force, shall be kept open while the ships are at sea;

.1.2.2 any operation of valves referred to in paragraph 6.1.4.1.2.1 shall be recorded in the log-book;

* Refer to Drainage of fire-fighting water from enclosed vehicle and ro–ro spaces and special category spaces for passenger and cargo ships (MSC.1/Circ.1234).

.1.3 in the spaces below the bulkhead deck, the Administration may require pumping and drainage facilities to be provided additional to the requirements of regulation II-1/35-1. In such case, the drainage system shall be sized to remove no less than 125% of the combined capacity of both the water-spraying system pumps and the required number of fire hose nozzles, taking into account the guidelines developed by the Organization.* The drainage system valves shall be operable from outside the protected space at a position in the vicinity of the extinguishing system controls. Bilge wells shall be of sufficient holding capacity and shall be arranged at the side shell of the ship at a distance from each other of not more than 40 m in each watertight compartment;

.2 in cargo ships, the drainage and pumping arrangements shall be such as to prevent the build-up of free surfaces. In such case, the drainage system shall be sized to remove no less than 125% of the combined capacity of both the water-spraying system pumps and the required number of fire hose nozzles, taking into account the guidelines developed by the Organization.* The drainage system valves shall be operable from outside the protected space at a position in the vicinity of the extinguishing system controls. Bilge wells shall be of sufficient holding capacity and shall be arranged at the side shell of the ship at a distance from each other of not more than 40 m in each watertight compartment. If this is not possible, the adverse effect upon stability of the added weight and free surface of water shall be taken into account to the extent deemed necessary by the Administration in its approval of the stability information.† Such information shall be included in the stability information supplied to the master as required by regulation II-1/5-1.

6.1.5 On all ships, for closed vehicles and ro–ro spaces and special category spaces, where fixed pressure water-spraying systems are fitted, means shall be provided to prevent the blockage of drainage arrangements, taking into account the guidelines developed by the Organization.* Ships constructed before 1 January 2010 shall comply with the requirements of this paragraph by the first survey after 1 January 2010."

* Refer to Drainage of fire-fighting water from enclosed vehicle and ro–ro spaces and special category spaces for passenger and cargo ships (MSC.1/Circ.1234).

† Refer to the Recommendation on fixed fire-extinguishing systems for special category spaces, adopted by the Organization by resolution A.123(V).

Chapter III
Life-saving appliances and arrangements

Regulation 6
Communications

6 *The existing paragraph 2.2 is replaced by the following:*

"**2.2** *Search and rescue locating devices*

At least one search and rescue locating device shall be carried on each side of every passenger ship and of every cargo ship of 500 gross tonnage and upwards. At least one search and rescue locating device shall be carried on every cargo ship of 300 gross tonnage and upwards but less than 500 gross tonnage. Such search and rescue locating devices shall conform to the applicable performance standards not inferior to those adopted by the Organization.* The search and rescue locating devices† shall be stowed in such location that they can be rapidly placed in any survival craft other than the liferaft or liferafts required by regulation 31.1.4. Alternatively one search and rescue locating device shall be stowed in each survival craft other than those required by regulation 31.1.4. On ships carrying at least two search and rescue locating devices and equipped with free-fall lifeboats one of the search and rescue locating devices shall be stowed in a free-fall lifeboat and the other located in the immediate vicinity of the navigation bridge so that it can be utilized on board and ready for transfer to any of the other survival craft.

* Refer to the Recommendation on performance standards for survival craft radar transponders for use in search and rescue operations, adopted by the Organization by resolution MSC.247(83) (A.802(19), as amended) and the Recommendation on performance standards for survival craft AIS Search and Rescue Transmitters (AIS-SART) for use in search and rescue operations, adopted by the Organization by resolution MSC.246(83).

† One of these search and rescue locating devices may be the search and rescue locating device required by regulation IV/7.1.3."

Regulation 26
Additional requirements for ro-ro passenger ships

7 *The existing paragraph 2.5 is replaced by the following:*

"**2.5** Liferafts carried on ro–ro passenger ships shall be fitted with a search and rescue locating device in the ratio of one search and rescue locating device for every four liferafts. The search and rescue locating device shall be mounted inside the liferaft so its antenna is more than one metre above the sea level when the liferaft is deployed, except that for canopied reversible liferafts the search and rescue locating device shall be so arranged as to be readily accessed and erected by survivors. Each search and rescue locating device shall be arranged to be manually erected when the liferaft is deployed. Containers of liferafts fitted with search and rescue locating devices shall be clearly marked."

Chapter IV
Radiocommunications

Regulation 7
Radio equipment: General

8 *In paragraph 1, subparagraph .3 is replaced by the following:*

"**.3** a search and rescue locating device capable of operating either in the 9 GHz band or on frequencies dedicated for AIS, which:"

Appendix
Certificates

Record of Equipment for the Passenger Ship Safety Certificate (Form P)

9 *In the Record of Equipment for the Passenger Ship Safety Certificate (Form P), in section 2, the existing item 11.1 is replaced by the following:*

"11.1 Number of search and rescue locating devices

11.1.1 Radar search and rescue transponders (SART)

11.1.2 AIS search and rescue transmitters (AIS-SART)",

and in section 3, the existing item 6 is replaced by the following:

"6 Ship's search and rescue locating device

6.1 Radar search and rescue transponder (SART)

6.2 AIS search and rescue transmitter (AIS-SART)".

Record of Equipment for the Cargo Ship Safety Equipment Certificate (Form E)

10 *In the Record of Equipment for the Cargo Ship Safety Equipment Certificate (Form E), in section 2, the existing item 9.1 is replaced by the following:*

"9.1 Number of search and rescue locating devices

9.1.1 Radar search and rescue transponders (SART)

9.1.2 AIS search and rescue transmitters (AIS-SART)".

Record of Equipment for the Cargo Ship Safety Radio Certificate (Form R)

11 *In the Record of Equipment for the Cargo Ship Safety Radio Certificate (Form R), in section 2, the existing item 6 is replaced by the following:*

"6 Ship's search and rescue locating device

6.1 Radar search and rescue transponder (SART)

6.2 AIS search and rescue transmitter (AIS-SART)".

Record of Equipment for the Nuclear Passenger Ship Safety Certificate (Form PNUC)

12 *In the Record of Equipment for the Nuclear Passenger Ship Safety Certificate (Form PNUC), in section 2, the existing item 11.1 is replaced by the following:*

"11.1 Number of search and rescue locating devices

11.1.1 Radar search and rescue transponders (SART)

11.1.2 AIS search and rescue transmitters (AIS-SART)",

and in section 3, the existing item 6 is replaced by the following:

"6 Ship's search and rescue locating device

6.1 Radar search and rescue transponder (SART)

6.2 AIS search and rescue transmitter (AIS-SART)".

Record of Equipment for the Nuclear Cargo Ship Safety Certificate (Form CNUC)

13 *In the Record of Equipment for the Nuclear Cargo Ship Safety Certificate (Form CNUC), in section 2, item 9 is deleted and items 10, 10.1 and 10.2 are renumbered as items 9, 9.1 and 9.2 respectively; and the renumbered item 9.1 is replaced by the following:*

"9.1 Number of search and rescue locating devices

9.1.1 Radar search and rescue transponders (SART)

9.1.2 AIS search and rescue transmitters (AIS-SART)",

and in section 3, the existing item 6 is replaced by the following:

"6 Ship's search and rescue locating device

6.1 Radar search and rescue transponder (SART)

6.2 AIS search and rescue transmitter (AIS-SART)".

Resolution MSC.257(84)

(adopted on 16 May 2008)

Adoption of amendments to the International Convention for the Safety of Life at Sea, 1974, as amended

THE MARITIME SAFETY COMMITTEE,

RECALLING Article 28(b) of the Convention on the International Maritime Organization concerning the functions of the Committee,

RECALLING FURTHER article VIII(b) of the International Convention for the Safety of Life at Sea (SOLAS), 1974 (hereinafter referred to as "the Convention"), concerning the amendment procedure applicable to the Annex to the Convention, other than to the provisions of chapter I thereof,

HAVING CONSIDERED, at its eighty-fourth session, amendments to the Convention, proposed and circulated in accordance with article VIII(b)(i) thereof,

1. ADOPTS, in accordance with article VIII(b)(iv) of the Convention, amendments to the Convention, the text of which is set out in the annex to the present resolution;

2. DETERMINES, in accordance with article VIII(b)(vi)(2)(bb) of the Convention, that the said amendments shall be deemed to have been accepted on 1 July 2009, unless, prior to that date, more than one third of the Contracting Governments to the Convention or Contracting Governments the combined merchant fleets of which constitute not less than 50% of the gross tonnage of the world's merchant fleet, have notified their objections to the amendments;

3. INVITES SOLAS Contracting Governments to note that, in accordance with article VIII(b)(vii)(2) of the Convention, the amendments shall enter into force on 1 January 2010 upon their acceptance in accordance with paragraph 2 above;

4. REQUESTS the Secretary-General, in conformity with article VIII(b)(v) of the Convention, to transmit certified copies of the present resolution

and the text of the amendments contained in the annex to all Contracting Governments to the Convention;

5. FURTHER REQUESTS the Secretary-General to transmit copies of this resolution and its annex to Members of the Organization, which are not Contracting Governments to the Convention.

Annex

Amendments to the International Convention for the Safety of Life at Sea, 1974, as amended

Chapter XI-1
Special measures to enhance maritime safety

1 *The following new regulation 6 is added after the existing regulation 5:*

"Regulation 6
Additional requirements for the investigation of marine casualties and incidents

Taking into account regulation I/21, each Administration shall conduct investigations of marine casualties and incidents, in accordance with the provisions of the present Convention, as supplemented by the provisions of the Code of the International Standards and Recommended Practices for a Safety Investigation into a Marine Casualty or Marine Incident (Casualty Investigation Code) adopted by resolution MSC.255(84), and:

.1 the provisions of parts I and II of the Casualty Investigation Code shall be fully complied with;

.2 the related guidance and explanatory material contained in part III of the Casualty Investigation Code should be taken into account to the greatest possible extent in order to achieve a more uniform implementation of the Casualty Investigation Code;

.3 amendments to parts I and II of the Casualty Investigation Code shall be adopted, brought into force and take effect in accordance with the provisions of article VIII of the present Convention concerning the amendment procedures applicable to the annex other than chapter I; and

.4 part III of the Casualty Investigation Code shall be amended by the Maritime Safety Committee in accordance with its rules of procedure."

Resolution MSC.258(84)
(adopted on 16 May 2008)

Adoption of amendments to the Protocol of 1988 relating to the International Convention for the Safety of Life at Sea, 1974

THE MARITIME SAFETY COMMITTEE,

RECALLING Article 28(b) of the Convention on the International Maritime Organization concerning the functions of the Committee,

RECALLING FURTHER article VIII(b) of the International Convention for the Safety of Life at Sea (SOLAS), 1974 (hereinafter referred to as "the Convention") and article VI of the Protocol of 1988 relating to the Convention (hereinafter referred to as "the 1988 SOLAS Protocol") concerning the procedure for amending the 1988 SOLAS Protocol,

HAVING CONSIDERED, at its eighty-fourth session, amendments to the 1988 SOLAS Protocol proposed and circulated in accordance with article VIII(b)(i) of the Convention and article VI of the 1988 SOLAS Protocol,

1. ADOPTS, in accordance with article VIII(b)(iv) of the Convention and article VI of the 1988 SOLAS Protocol, amendments to the appendix to the Annex to the 1988 SOLAS Protocol, the text of which is set out in the annex to the present resolution;

2. DETERMINES, in accordance with article VIII(b)(vi)(2)(bb) of the Convention and article VI of the 1988 SOLAS Protocol, that the said amendments shall be deemed to have been accepted on 1 July 2009, unless, prior to that date, more than one third of the Parties to the 1988 SOLAS Protocol or Parties the combined merchant fleets of which constitute not less than 50% of the gross tonnage of the world's merchant fleet, have notified their objections to the amendments;

3. INVITES the Parties concerned to note that, in accordance with article VIII(b)(vii)(2) of the Convention and article VI of the 1988 SOLAS Protocol, the amendments shall enter into force on 1 January 2010, upon their acceptance in accordance with paragraph 2 above;

4. RECOMMENDS the Parties concerned to issue certificates complying with the annexed amendments at the first renewal survey on or after 1 January 2010;

5. REQUESTS the Secretary-General, in conformity with article VIII(b)(v) of the Convention and article VI of the 1988 SOLAS Protocol, to transmit certified copies of the present resolution and the text of the amendments contained in the annex to all Parties to the 1988 SOLAS Protocol;

6. FURTHER REQUESTS the Secretary-General to transmit copies of this resolution and its annex to Members of the Organization, which are not Parties to the 1988 SOLAS Protocol.

Annex

Amendments to the Protocol of 1988 relating to the International Convention for the Safety of Life at Sea, 1974, as amended

Annex

Modifications and additions to the Annex to the International Convention for the Safety of Life at Sea, 1974

Appendix

Modifications and additions to the appendix to the Annex to the International Convention for the Safety of Life at Sea, 1974

Record of Equipment for the Passenger Ship Safety Certificate (Form P)

1 *In the Record of Equipment for the Passenger Ship Safety Certificate (Form P), in section 2, the existing item 11.1 is replaced by the following:*

"11.1 Number of search and rescue locating devices

11.1.1 Radar search and rescue transponders (SART)

11.1.2 AIS search and rescue transmitters (AIS-SART)",

and in section 3, the existing item 6 is replaced by the following:

"6 Ship's search and rescue locating device

6.1 Radar search and rescue transponder (SART)

6.2 AIS search and rescue transmitter (AIS-SART)".

Record of Equipment for the Cargo Ship Safety Equipment Certificate (Form E)

2 *In the Record of Equipment for the Cargo Ship Safety Equipment Certificate (Form E), in section 2, the existing item 9.1 is replaced by the following:*

"9.1 Number of search and rescue locating devices

9.1.1 Radar search and rescue transponders (SART)

9.1.2 AIS search and rescue transmitters (AIS-SART)".

Record of Equipment for the Cargo Ship Safety Radio Certificate (Form R)

3 *In the Record of Equipment for the Cargo Ship Safety Radio Certificate (Form R), in section 2, the existing item 6 is replaced by the following:*

"6 Ship's search and rescue locating device

6.1 Radar search and rescue transponder (SART)

6.2 AIS search and rescue transmitter (AIS-SART)".

Record of Equipment for the Cargo Ship Safety Certificate (Form C)

4 *In the Record of Equipment for the Cargo Ship Safety Certificate (Form C), in section 2, the existing item 9.1 is replaced by the following:*

"9.1 Number of search and rescue locating devices

9.1.1 Radar search and rescue transponders (SART)

9.1.2 AIS search and rescue transmitters (AIS-SART)",

and in section 3, the existing item 6 is replaced by the following:

"6 Ship's search and rescue locating device

6.1 Radar search and rescue transponder (SART)

6.2 AIS search and rescue transmitter (AIS-SART)".

Resolution MSC.269(85)
(adopted on 4 December 2008)

Adoption of amendments to the International Convention for the Safety of Life at Sea, 1974, as amended

THE MARITIME SAFETY COMMITTEE,

RECALLING Article 28(b) of the Convention on the International Maritime Organization concerning the functions of the Committee,

RECALLING FURTHER article VIII(b) of the International Convention for the Safety of Life at Sea (SOLAS), 1974 (hereinafter referred to as "the Convention"), concerning the amendment procedure applicable to the Annex to the Convention, other than to the provisions of chapter I thereof,

HAVING CONSIDERED, at its eighty-fifth session, amendments to the Convention, proposed and circulated in accordance with article VIII(b)(i) thereof,

1. ADOPTS, in accordance with article VIII(b)(iv) of the Convention, amendments to the Convention, the text of which is set out in annexes 1 and 2 to the present resolution;

2. DETERMINES, in accordance with article VIII(b)(vi)(2)(bb) of the Convention, that:

(a) the said amendments, set out in annex 1, shall be deemed to have been accepted on 1 January 2010; and

(b) the said amendments, set out in annex 2, shall be deemed to have been accepted on 1 July 2010,

unless, prior to those dates, more than one third of the Contracting Governments to the Convention or Contracting Governments, the combined merchant fleets of which constitute not less than 50% of the gross tonnage of the world's merchant fleet, have notified their objections to the amendments;

3. INVITES Contracting Governments to the Convention to note that, in accordance with article VIII(b)(vii)(2) of the Convention:

(a) the amendments, set out in annex 1, shall enter into force on 1 July 2010; and

(b) the amendments, set out in annex 2, shall enter into force on 1 January 2011,

upon their acceptance in accordance with paragraph 2 above;

4. REQUESTS the Secretary-General, in conformity with article VIII(b)(v) of the Convention, to transmit certified copies of the present resolution and the text of the amendments contained in annexes 1 and 2 to all Contracting Governments to the Convention;

5. FURTHER REQUESTS the Secretary-General to transmit copies of this resolution and its annexes 1 and 2 to Members of the Organization, which are not Contracting Governments to the Convention.

Annex 1

Amendments to the International Convention for the Safety of Life at Sea, 1974, as amended

Chapter II-1
Construction – Structure, subdivision and stability, machinery and electrical installations

Part A
General

Regulation 2
Definitions

1 *The following new paragraph 27 is added after the existing paragraph 26:*

"**27** *2008 IS Code* means the International Code on Intact Stability, 2008, consisting of an introduction, part A (the provisions of which shall be treated as mandatory) and part B (the provisions of which shall be treated as recommendatory), as adopted by resolution MSC.267(85), provided that:

.1 amendments to the introduction and part A of the Code are adopted, brought into force and take effect in accordance with the provisions of article VIII of the present Convention concerning the amendment procedures applicable to the Annex other than chapter I thereof; and

.2 amendments to part B of the Code are adopted by the Maritime Safety Committee in accordance with its Rules of Procedure."

Part B-1
Stability

Regulation 5
Intact stability information

2 *In the existing title of the regulation, the word "*information*" is deleted.*

3 *In paragraph 1, the following new sentence is added after the existing sentence:*

"In addition to any other applicable requirements of the present regulations, ships having a length of 24 m and upwards constructed on or after 1 July 2010 shall as a minimum comply with the requirements of part A of the 2008 IS Code."

Chapter II-2
Construction – Fire protection, fire detection and fire extinction

Part A
General

Regulation 1
Application

4 *The following new paragraph 2.3 is added:*

"**2.3** Ships constructed on or after 1 July 2002 and before 1 July 2010 shall comply with paragraphs 7.1.1, 7.4.4.2, 7.4.4.3 and 7.5.2.1.2 of regulation 9, as adopted by resolution MSC.99(73)."

Part C
Suppression of fire

Regulation 9
Containment of fire

5 *The last sentence of paragraph 4.1.1.2 is moved to a new separate paragraph 4.1.1.3 and the existing following paragraphs are renumbered accordingly.*

6 *The following text is added at the end of paragraph 4.1.1.2:*

"Doors approved without the sill being part of the frame, which are installed on or after 1 July 2010, shall be installed such that the gap under the door does not exceed 12 mm. A non-combustible sill shall be installed under the door such that floor coverings do not extend beneath the closed door."

7 *The following text is added at the end of paragraph 4.1.2.1:*

"Doors approved without the sill being part of the frame, which are installed on or after 1 July 2010, shall be installed such that the gap under the door does not exceed 25 mm."

8 *In paragraph 4.2.1, the following text is added after the first sentence:*

"Doors approved as "A" class without the sill being part of the frame, which are installed on or after 1 July 2010, shall be installed such that the gap under the door does not exceed 12 mm and a non-combustible sill shall be installed under the door such that floor coverings do not extend beneath the closed door. Doors approved as "B" class without the sill being part of the frame, which are installed on or after 1 July 2010, shall be installed such that the gap under the door does not exceed 25 mm."

9 *In paragraph 7.1.1, in the first and second sentences, the word* "non-combustible" *is replaced by the words* "steel or equivalent".

10 *At the beginning of paragraph 7.1.1.1, the words* "subject to paragraph 7.1.1.2" *are added and the word* "a" *before the word* "material" *is replaced by the word* "any".

11 *The following new subparagraph .2 is added after the existing paragraph 7.1.1.1 and the existing subsequent subparagraphs are renumbered accordingly:*

"**.2** on ships constructed on or after 1 July 2010, the ducts shall be made of heat resisting non-combustible material, which may be faced internally and externally with membranes having low flame-spread characteristics and, in each case, a calorific value* not exceeding 45 MJ/m^2 of their surface area for the thickness used;

* Refer to the recommendations published by the International Organization for Standardization, in particular publication ISO 1716:2002, *Reaction to fire tests for building products – Determination of the heat of combustion."*

12 *In paragraph 7.4.4.2, the word* "non-combustible" *is replaced by the words* "steel or equivalent".

13 *In paragraph 7.4.4.3, the word* "non-combustible" *is replaced by the words* "steel or equivalent".

14 *At the beginning of paragraph 7.4.4.3.1, the words* "subject to paragraph 7.4.4.3.2" *are added and the word* "a" *before the word* "material" *is replaced by the word* "any".

15 *The following new subparagraph .3.2 is added after the existing paragraph 7.4.4.3.1 and the existing subsequent subparagraphs are renumbered accordingly:*

".**3.2** on ships constructed on or after 1 July 2010, the ducts shall be made of heat resisting non-combustible material, which may be faced internally and externally with membranes having low flame-spread characteristics and, in each case, a calorific value* not exceeding 45 MJ/m^2 of their surface area for the thickness used;

* Refer to the recommendations published by the International Organization for Standardization, in particular publication ISO 1716:2002, *Reaction to fire tests for building products – Determination of the heat of combustion."*

16 *At the end of paragraph 7.5.2.1.2, the words* "and, in addition, a fire damper in the upper end of the duct" *are added.*

Regulation 10
Fire fighting

17 *The following new paragraph 10.2.6 is inserted after the existing paragraph 10.2.5:*

"**10.2.6** Passenger ships carrying more than 36 passengers constructed on or after 1 July 2010 shall be fitted with a suitably located means for fully recharging breathing air cylinders, free from contamination. The means for recharging shall be either:

.1 breathing air compressors supplied from the main and emergency switchboard, or independently driven, with a minimum capacity of 60 *l*/min per required breathing apparatus, not to exceed 420 *l*/min; or

.2 self-contained high-pressure storage systems of suitable pressure to recharge the breathing apparatus used on board, with a capacity of at least 1,200 *l* per required breathing apparatus, not to exceed 50,000 *l* of free air."

Annex 2

Amendments to the International Convention for the Safety of Life at Sea, 1974, as amended

Chapter II-2
Construction – Fire protection, fire detection and fire extinction

Part A
General

Regulation 1
Application

1 *The following new paragraph 2.4 is added after the existing paragraph 2.3:*

"**2.4** The following ships, with cargo spaces intended for the carriage of packaged dangerous goods, shall comply with regulation 19.3, except when carrying dangerous goods specified as classes 6.2 and 7 and dangerous goods in limited quantities* and excepted quantities† in accordance with tables 19.1 and 19.3, not later than the date of the first renewal survey on or after 1 January 2011:

.1 cargo ships of 500 gross tonnage and upwards and passenger ships constructed on or after 1 September 1984 but before 1 January 2011; and

.2 cargo ships of less than 500 gross tonnage constructed on or after 1 February 1992 but before 1 January 2011,

and notwithstanding these provisions:

.3 cargo ships of 500 gross tonnage and upwards and passenger ships constructed on or after 1 September 1984 but before

* Refer to chapter 3.4 of the IMDG Code.

† Refer to chapter 3.5 of the IMDG Code.

1 July 1986 need not comply with regulation 19.3.3 provided that they comply with regulation 54.2.3 as adopted by resolution MSC.1(XLV);

.4 cargo ships of 500 gross tonnage and upwards and passenger ships constructed on or after 1 July 1986 but before 1 February 1992 need not comply with regulation 19.3.3 provided that they comply with regulation 54.2.3 as amended by resolution MSC.6(48);

.5 cargo ships of 500 gross tonnage and upwards and passenger ships constructed on or after 1 September 1984 but before 1 July 1998 need not comply with regulations 19.3.10.1 and 19.3.10.2; and

.6 cargo ships of less than 500 gross tonnage constructed on or after 1 February 1992 but before 1 July 1998 need not comply with regulations 19.3.10.1 and 19.3.10.2."

Part E
Operational requirements

Regulation 16
Operations

2 *In paragraph 2.1, the reference to "*the Code of Safe Practice for Solid Bulk Cargoes*" is replaced by the reference to "*the International Maritime Solid Bulk Cargoes (IMSBC) Code*".*

Part G
Special requirements

Regulation 19
Carriage of dangerous goods

3 *The existing note 1 to table 19.1 is replaced by the following:*

"1 For classes 4 and 5.1 solids not applicable to closed freight containers. For classes 2, 3, 6.1 and 8 when carried in closed freight containers, the ventilation rate may be reduced to not less than two air changes per hour. For classes 4 and 5.1 liquids when carried in closed freight containers, the ventilation rate may be reduced to not less than two air changes per hour. For the purpose of this requirement, a portable tank is a closed freight container."

4 *In note 10 to table 19.2, the words* "the Code of Safe Practice for Solid Bulk Cargoes, adopted by resolution A.434(XI)" *are replaced by the words* "the International Maritime Solid Bulk Cargoes (IMSBC) Code".

5 *The existing table 19.3 is replaced by the following table:*

"**Table 19.3 – Application of the requirements to different classes of dangerous goods except solid dangerous goods in bulk**

Regulation 19 \ Class	1.1 to 1.6	1.4S	2.1	2.2	2.3 flammable[20]	2.3 non-flammable	3 FP[15] < 23°C	3 FP[15] ≥ 23°C to ≤ 60°C	4.1	4.2	4.3 liquids[21]	4.3 solids	5.1	5.2[16]	6.1 liquids FP[15] < 23°C	6.1 liquids FP[15] ≥ 23°C to ≤ 60°C	6.1 liquids	6.1 solids	8 liquids FP[15] < 23°C	8 liquids FP[15] ≥ 23°C to ≤ 60°C	8 liquids	8 solids	9
.3.1.1	X	X	X	X	X	X	X	X	X	X	X	X	X	X	X	X	X	X	X	X	X	X	X
.3.1.2	X	X	X	X	X	X	X	X	X	X	X	X	X	X	X	X	X	X	X	X	X	X	–
.3.1.3	X	–	–	–	–	–	–	–	–	–	–	–	–	–	–	–	–	–	–	–	–	–	–
.3.1.4	X	–	–	–	–	–	–	–	–	–	–	–	–	–	–	–	–	–	–	–	–	–	–
.3.2	X	–	X	–	X	–	X	–	–	–	X[18]	–	–	–	X	–	–	–	X	–	–	–	X[17]
.3.3	X	X	X	X	–	X	X	X	X	X	X	X	X	–	X	X	X	X	X	X	X	X	–
.3.4.1	–	–	X	–	–	X	X	–	X[11]	X[11]	X	X	X[11]	–	X	X	–	X[11]	X	X	–	–	X[11]
.3.4.2	–	–	X	–	–	–	X	–	–	–	–	–	–	–	X	–	–	–	X	–	–	–	X[17]
.3.5	–	–	–	–	–	–	X	–	–	–	–	–	–	–	X	X	X	–	X	X[19]	X[19]	–	–
.3.6	–	–	X	X	X	X	X	X	X	X	X	X	X	X	X	X	X	X	X	X	X	X	X[14]
.3.7	–	–	–	–	–	–	X	X	X	X	X	X	X	–	X	X	–	–	X	X	–	–	–
.3.8	X[12]	–	X	X	X	X	X	X	X	X	X	X	X[13]	X	X	X	–	–	X	X	–	–	–
.3.9	X	X	X	X	X	X	X	X	X	X	X	X	X	X	X	X	X	X	X	X	X	X	X
.3.10.1	X	X	X	X	X	X	X	X	X	X	X	X	X	X	X	X	X	X	X	X	X	X	X
.3.10.2	X	X	X	X	X	X	X	X	X	X	X	X	X	X	X	X	X	X	X	X	X	X	X

11 When "mechanically-ventilated spaces" are required by the IMDG Code.
12 Stow 3 m horizontally away from the machinery space boundaries in all cases.
13 Refer to the IMDG Code.
14 As appropriate for the goods to be carried.
15 FP means flashpoint.
16 Under the provisions of the IMDG Code, stowage of class 5.2 dangerous goods under deck or in enclosed ro–ro spaces is prohibited.
17 Only applicable to dangerous goods evolving flammable vapour listed in the IMDG Code.
18 Only applicable to dangerous goods having a flashpoint less than 23°C listed in the IMDG Code.
19 Only applicable to dangerous goods having a subsidiary risk class 6.1.
20 Under the provisions of the IMDG Code, stowage of class 2.3 having subsidiary risk class 2.1 under deck or in enclosed ro–ro spaces is prohibited.
21 Under the provisions of the IMDG Code, stowage of class 4.3 liquids having a flashpoint less than 23°C under deck or in enclosed ro–ro spaces is prohibited."

6 *In paragraph 2.1, after the words* "except when carrying dangerous goods in limited quantities"*, the following words are added:*

"and excepted quantities*

* Refer to chapter 3.5 of the IMDG Code.".

7 *In paragraph 3.4, the existing title is replaced as follows:*

"**3.4** *Ventilation arrangement*".

8 *The following text is added at the end of the first sentence of paragraph 3.6.1:*

"and shall be selected taking into account the hazards associated with the chemicals being transported and the standards developed by the Organization according to the class and physical state.*

* For solid bulk cargoes, the protective clothing should satisfy the equipment provisions specified in the respective schedules of the IMSBC Code for the individual substances. For packaged goods, the protective clothing should satisfy the equipment provisions specified in emergency procedures (EmS) of the Supplement to the IMDG Code for the individual substances."

9 *At the end of paragraph 4, the words* "and excepted quantities" *are added.*

Chapter VI
Carriage of cargoes

Part A
General provisions

10 *The following new regulations 1-1 and 1-2 are added after the existing regulation 1:*

"Regulation 1-1
Definitions

For the purpose of this chapter, unless expressly provided otherwise, the following definitions shall apply:

1 *IMSBC Code* means the International Maritime Solid Bulk Cargoes (IMSBC) Code adopted by the Maritime Safety Committee of the Organization by resolution MSC.268(85), as may be amended by the Organization, provided that such amendments are adopted, brought into force and take effect in accordance with the provisions of article VIII of the present Convention concerning the amendment procedures applicable to the Annex other than chapter I.

2 *Solid bulk cargo* means any cargo, other than liquid or gas, consisting of a combination of particles, granules or any larger pieces of material generally uniform in composition, which is loaded directly into the cargo spaces of a ship without any intermediate form of containment.

Regulation 1-2
Requirements for the carriage of solid bulk cargoes other than grain

The carriage of solid bulk cargoes other than grain shall be in compliance with the relevant provisions of the IMSBC Code."

Regulation 2
Cargo information

11 *The existing subparagraph .2 of paragraph 2 is replaced by the following:*

> "**.2** in the case of solid bulk cargo, information as required by section 4 of the IMSBC Code."

12 *The existing paragraph 2.3 is deleted.*

Regulation 3
Oxygen analysis and gas detection equipment

13 *In paragraph 1, the word* "solid" *is inserted in the first sentence, after the words* "When transporting a".

Part B
Special provisions for bulk cargoes other than grain

14 *The title of part B is replaced as follows:*

"Special provisions for solid bulk cargoes".

Regulation 6
Acceptability for shipment

15 *In existing paragraph 1, the word* "solid" *is inserted in the first sentence after the words* "Prior to loading a".

16 *The existing paragraphs 2 and 3 are deleted.*

Regulation 7
Loading, unloading and stowage of bulk cargoes

17 *In the heading of the regulation, the word* "solid" *is inserted after the words* "stowage of".

18 *The existing paragraphs 4 and 5 are deleted and the subsequent paragraphs are renumbered accordingly.*

Chapter VII
Carriage of dangerous goods

Part A-1
Carriage of dangerous goods in solid form in bulk

Regulation 7-1
Application

19 *In paragraph 3 of the regulation, the words* "detailed instructions on the safe carriage of dangerous goods in solid form in bulk which shall include" *are deleted.*

20 *The following new regulation 7-5 is inserted after regulation 7-4:*

"Regulation 7-5
Requirements for the carriage of dangerous goods in solid form in bulk

The carriage of dangerous goods in solid form in bulk shall be in compliance with the relevant provisions of the IMSBC Code, as defined in regulation VI/1-1.1."

2009 amendments

Resolution MSC.282(86)

(adopted on 5 June 2009)

Adoption of amendments to the International Convention for the Safety of Life at Sea, 1974, as amended

THE MARITIME SAFETY COMMITTEE,

RECALLING Article 28(b) of the Convention on the International Maritime Organization concerning the functions of the Committee,

RECALLING FURTHER article VIII(b) of the International Convention for the Safety of Life at Sea (SOLAS), 1974 (hereinafter referred to as "the Convention"), concerning the amendment procedure applicable to the Annex to the Convention, other than to the provisions of chapter I thereof,

HAVING CONSIDERED, at its eighty-sixth session, amendments to the Convention, proposed and circulated in accordance with article VIII(b)(i) thereof,

1. ADOPTS, in accordance with article VIII(b)(iv) of the Convention, amendments to the Convention, the text of which is set out in the annex to the present resolution;

2. DETERMINES, in accordance with article VIII(b)(vi)(2)(bb) of the Convention, that the said amendments shall be deemed to have been accepted on 1 July 2010, unless, prior to that date, more than one third of the Contracting Governments to the Convention or Contracting Governments the combined merchant fleets of which constitute not less than 50% of the gross tonnage of the world's merchant fleet, have notified their objections to the amendments;

3. INVITES SOLAS Contracting Governments to note that, in accordance with article VIII(b)(vii)(2) of the Convention, the amendments shall enter into force on 1 January 2011 upon their acceptance in accordance with paragraph 2 above;

4. REQUESTS the Secretary-General, in conformity with article VIII(b)(v) of the Convention, to transmit certified copies of the present resolution

and the text of the amendments contained in the annex to all Contracting Governments to the Convention;

5. FURTHER REQUESTS the Secretary-General to transmit copies of this resolution and its annex to Members of the Organization, which are not Contracting Governments to the Convention.

Annex

Amendments to the International Convention for the Safety of Life at Sea, 1974, as amended

Chapter II-1
Construction - Structure, subdivision and stability, machinery and electrical installations

Part A-1
Structure of ships

Regulation 3-5
New installation of materials containing asbestos

1 *The existing text of paragraph 2 is replaced by the following:*

"From 1 January 2011, for all ships, new installation of materials which contain asbestos shall be prohibited."

Part C
Machinery installations

Regulation 35-1
Bilge pumping arrangements

2 *The following new paragraph 2.6.3 is added after the existing paragraph 2.6.2:*

"**2.6.3** Provisions for the drainage of closed vehicle and ro–ro spaces and special category spaces shall also comply with regulations II-2/20.6.1.4 and II-2/20.6.1.5."

Chapter V
Safety of navigation

Regulation 19

Carriage requirements for shipborne navigational systems and equipment

3 *In paragraph 2.1, the existing subparagraph .4 is replaced by the following:*

"**.4** nautical charts and nautical publications to plan and display the ship's route for the intended voyage and to plot and monitor positions throughout the voyage. An electronic chart display and information system (ECDIS) is also accepted as meeting the chart carriage requirements of this subparagraph. Ships to which paragraph 2.10 applies shall comply with the carriage requirements for ECDIS detailed therein;".

4 *In paragraph 2.2, the new subparagraphs .3 and .4 are added after the existing subparagraph .2 as follows:*

"**.3** a bridge navigational watch alarm system (BNWAS), as follows:

.1 cargo ships of 150 gross tonnage and upwards and passenger ships irrespective of size constructed on or after 1 July 2011;

.2 passenger ships irrespective of size constructed before 1 July 2011, not later than the first survey* after 1 July 2012;

.3 cargo ships of 3,000 gross tonnage and upwards constructed before 1 July 2011, not later than the first survey* after 1 July 2012;

.4 cargo ships of 500 gross tonnage and upwards but less than 3,000 gross tonnage constructed before 1 July 2011, not later than the first survey* after 1 July 2013; and

.5 cargo ships of 150 gross tonnage and upwards but less than 500 gross tonnage constructed before 1 July 2011, not later than the first survey* after 1 July 2014.

---

* Refer to the Unified interpretation of the term "first survey" referred to in SOLAS regulations (MSC.1/Circ.1290).

The bridge navigational watch alarm system shall be in operation whenever the ship is underway at sea;

.4 a bridge navigational watch alarm system (BNWAS) installed prior to 1 July 2011 may subsequently be exempted from full compliance with the standards adopted by the Organization, at the discretion of the Administration."

5 *After the existing paragraph 2.9, the new paragraphs 2.10 and 2.11 are added as follows:*

"**2.10** Ships engaged on international voyages shall be fitted with an electronic chart display and information system (ECDIS) as follows:

.1 passenger ships of 500 gross tonnage and upwards constructed on or after 1 July 2012;

.2 tankers of 3,000 gross tonnage and upwards constructed on or after 1 July 2012;

.3 cargo ships, other than tankers, of 10,000 gross tonnage and upwards constructed on or after 1 July 2013;

.4 cargo ships, other than tankers, of 3,000 gross tonnage and upwards but less than 10,000 gross tonnage constructed on or after 1 July 2014;

.5 passenger ships of 500 gross tonnage and upwards constructed before 1 July 2012, not later than the first survey* on or after 1 July 2014;

.6 tankers of 3,000 gross tonnage and upwards constructed before 1 July 2012, not later than the first survey* on or after 1 July 2015;

.7 cargo ships, other than tankers, of 50,000 gross tonnage and upwards constructed before 1 July 2013, not later than the first survey* on or after 1 July 2016;

.8 cargo ships, other than tankers, of 20,000 gross tonnage and upwards but less than 50,000 gross tonnage constructed before 1 July 2013, not later than the first survey* on or after 1 July 2017; and

* Refer to the Unified interpretation of the term "first survey" referred to in SOLAS regulations (MSC.1/Circ.1290).

.9 cargo ships, other than tankers, of 10,000 gross tonnage and upwards but less than 20,000 gross tonnage constructed before 1 July 2013, not later than the first survey* on or after 1 July 2018.

2.11 Administrations may exempt ships from the application of the requirements of paragraph 2.10 when such ships will be taken permanently out of service within two years after the implementation date specified in subparagraphs .5 to .9 of paragraph 2.10.

* Refer to the Unified interpretation of the term "first survey" referred to in SOLAS regulations (MSC.1/Circ.1290)."

Chapter VI
Carriage of cargoes

6 *The title of chapter VI is replaced by the following:*

"Carriage of cargoes and oil fuels".

Regulation 1
Application

7 *At the beginning of paragraph 1, the words "*Unless expressly provided otherwise,*" are added and the existing word "*This*" is replaced by the word "*this*".*

Regulation 5-1
Material safety data sheets

8 *The existing text of the regulation is replaced by the following:*

"Ships carrying oil or oil fuel, as defined in regulation 1 of Annex I of the International Convention for the Prevention of Pollution from Ships, 1973, as modified by the Protocol of 1978 relating thereto, shall be provided with material safety data sheets, based on the recommendations developed by the Organization,* prior to the loading of such oil as cargo in bulk or bunkering of oil fuel.

* Refer to the Recommendations for material safety data sheets (MSDS) for MARPOL Annex I oil cargo and oil fuel, adopted by the Organization by resolution MSC.286(86), as may be amended."

Appendix
Certificates

Record of Equipment for the Passenger Ship Safety Certificate (Form P)

9 *In the Record of Equipment for the Passenger Ship Safety Certificate (Form P), in section 5, a new item 14 is inserted as follows:*

"14 Bridge navigational watch alarm system (BNWAS)".

Record of Equipment for the Cargo Ship Safety Equipment Certificate (Form E)

10 *In the Record of Equipment for the Cargo Ship Safety Equipment Certificate (Form E), in section 3, a new item 14 is inserted as follows:*

"14 Bridge navigational watch alarm system (BNWAS)".

Record of Equipment for the Nuclear Passenger Ship Safety Certificate (Form PNUC)

11 *In the Record of Equipment for the Nuclear Passenger Ship Safety Certificate (Form PNUC), in section 5, a new item 15 is inserted as follows:*

"15 Bridge navigational watch alarm system (BNWAS)".

Record of Equipment for the Nuclear Cargo Ship Safety Certificate (Form CNUC)

12 *In the Record of Equipment for the Nuclear Cargo Ship Safety Certificate (Form CNUC), in section 5, a new item 14 is inserted as follows:*

"14 Bridge navigational watch alarm system (BNWAS)".

Footnote to be added to SOLAS regulation V/18

In the existing footnote to paragraph 2, the following reference is added after the last reference:

"Performance standards for a bridge navigational watch alarm system (BNWAS) (resolution MSC.128(75))".

Resolution MSC.283(86)
(adopted on 5 June 2009)

Adoption of amendments to the Protocol of 1988 relating to the International Convention for the Safety of Life at Sea, 1974

THE MARITIME SAFETY COMMITTEE,

RECALLING Article 28(b) of the Convention on the International Maritime Organization concerning the functions of the Committee,

RECALLING FURTHER article VIII(b) of the International Convention for the Safety of Life at Sea (SOLAS), 1974 (hereinafter referred to as "the Convention") and article VI of the Protocol of 1988 relating to the Convention (hereinafter referred to as "the 1988 SOLAS Protocol") concerning the procedure for amending the 1988 SOLAS Protocol,

HAVING CONSIDERED, at its eighty-sixth session, amendments to the 1988 SOLAS Protocol in accordance with article VIII(b)(i) of the Convention and article VI of the 1988 SOLAS Protocol,

1. ADOPTS, in accordance with article VIII(b)(iv) of the Convention and article VI of the 1988 SOLAS Protocol, amendments to the appendix to the Annex to the 1988 SOLAS Protocol, the text of which is set out in the annex to the present resolution;

2. DETERMINES, in accordance with article VIII(b)(vi)(2)(bb) of the Convention and article VI of the 1988 SOLAS Protocol, that the said amendments shall be deemed to have been accepted on 1 July 2010, unless, prior to that date, more than one third of the Parties to the 1988 SOLAS Protocol or Parties the combined merchant fleets of which constitute not less than 50% of the gross tonnage of the world's merchant fleet, have notified their objections to the amendments;

3. INVITES the Parties concerned to note that, in accordance with article VIII(b)(vii)(2) of the Convention and article VI of the 1988 SOLAS Protocol, the amendments shall enter into force on 1 January 2011, upon their acceptance in accordance with paragraph 2 above;

4. REQUESTS the Secretary-General, in conformity with article VIII(b)(v) of the Convention and article VI of the 1988 SOLAS Protocol, to transmit certified copies of the present resolution and the text of the amendments contained in the annex to all Parties to the 1988 SOLAS Protocol;

5. FURTHER REQUESTS the Secretary-General to transmit copies of this resolution and its annex to Members of the Organization, which are not Parties to the 1988 SOLAS Protocol.

Annex

Amendments to the Protocol of 1988 relating to the International Convention for the Safety of Life at Sea, 1974, as amended

Annex

Modifications and additions to the Annex to the International Convention for the Safety of Life at Sea, 1974

Appendix

Modifications and additions to the appendix to the Annex to the International Convention for the Safety of Life at Sea, 1974

Record of Equipment for the Passenger Ship Safety Certificate (Form P)

1 *In the Record of Equipment for the Passenger Ship Safety Certificate (Form P), in section 5, a new item 14 is inserted as follows:*

"14 Bridge navigational watch alarm system (BNWAS)".

Record of Equipment for the Cargo Ship Safety Equipment Certificate (Form E)

2 *In the Record of Equipment for the Cargo Ship Safety Equipment Certificate (Form E), in section 3, a new item 14 is inserted as follows:*

"14 Bridge navigational watch alarm system (BNWAS)".

Record of Equipment for the Cargo Ship Safety Certificate (Form C)

3 *In the Record of Equipment for the Cargo Ship Safety Certificate (Form C), in section 5, a new item 15 is inserted as follows:*

"15 Bridge navigational watch alarm system (BNWAS)".

Related IMO Publishing titles

The following publications might be of interest to you. They may be purchased from authorized distributors. Please visit our website (www.imo.org) for further details.

SOLAS

(Consolidated edition, 2009)

Of all the international conventions dealing with maritime safety, the most important is the International Convention for the Safety of Life at Sea, 1974, as amended, better known as SOLAS, which covers a wide range of measures designed to improve the safety of shipping. In order to provide an easy reference to all SOLAS requirements applicable from 1 July 2009, this edition presents a consolidated text of the SOLAS Convention, its Protocols of 1978 and 1988 and all amendments in effect from that date.

Arabic	IE110A	ISBN	978-92-801-5218-0
Chinese	IE110C		978-92-801-6074-1
English	IE110E		978-92-801-1505-5
French	IE110F		978-92-801-2425-5
Russian	IE110R		978-92-801-4268-6
Spanish	IE110S		978-92-801-0198-0

SOLAS on CD (V7.0)

(2009 edition)

This CD provides a consolidated text of the SOLAS Convention, its Protocols of 1978 and 1988 and amendments in force as on 1 July 2009. A comprehensive cross-referencing and indexing system allows the user to navigate easily between the provisions of the Convention, its annex and related texts. Pages of the text and of the on-screen manual can be printed out.

English DG110E ISBN 978-92-801-7029-0

SOLAS on the Web

This is a yearly subscription to the SOLAS Convention. It is regularly updated and contains existing SOLAS amendments and amendments not yet in force.

It provides users with access to:

- Logical and easy-to-understand indexes
- Cross referencing with hundreds of internal links
- Clear tables for easy reference

English S110E

Visit www.imo.org for your local distributor

4 Albert Embankment • London SE1 7SR • United Kingdom
Tel: +44 (0)20 7735 7611 • Fax: +44 (0)20 7587 3241
Email: sales@imo.org
www.imo.org

Notes

Notes

Notes

Notes

Notes

Notes

Notes

Notes

Notes